JERALD SIMON

I0167345

Sand Castles

*10 Soothing New Age and contemporary pieces
for intermediate - late intermediate piano students*

MUSIC MENTOR

JERALD SIMON

Music Motivation®
Cool music that excites, entertains, and educates!

visit http://musicmotivation.com
follow Jerald on Facebook: https://facebook.com/jeraldsimon
subscribe to Jerald's YouTube page: https://youtube.com/jeraldsimon

Music Motivation® books are designed to provide students with music instruction that will enable them to improve and increase their successes in the field of music. It is also intended to enhance appreciation and understanding of various styles of music from classical to jazz, blues, rock, popular, new age, hymns, and more. The author and publisher disclaim any liability or accountability for the misuse of this material as it was intended by the author.

Copyright © 2017 by **Music Motivation**® - All Rights Reserved - International Copyright Secured.
WARNING: The music, text, design, and graphics in this publication are protected by copyright law.
Any duplication in any form for any purpose is an infringement of U.S. copyright law.

I hope you enjoy "Sand Castles." With this book, I hope that piano teachers and piano students have fun! Each "Cool Song" teaches the theory, concept, or skill for which they were created. More important, I want the students to have a good time playing these. These are great as student savers and very fun performance pieces any student would want to play and perform. Minus tracks can be used as well. You will hear the accompaniment music at three speeds: (1) Performance Speed with Piano, (2) Performance Speed - No Piano, and (3) Practice Speed - No Piano.

Your Music Mentor Jerald Simon

This book is dedicated to the many YouTube subscribers who watch my videos on my YouTube page (youtube.com/jeraldsimon) Also, for my wife, Suzanne (Zanny), my sweet daughter, Summer, and my two sons, Preston, and Matthew.

The family portrait on the back cover was shot by Wendy Santiano. Visit her website at:

http://www.wendysantiano.com or
https://www.facebook.com/wsantianoauthor

The front and background image is a photo taken by Jerald Simon. Jerald publishes his own photography in a book series titled: "Motivation in a Minute" featuring motivational messages he has written to go along with his photography.

CONNECT with Jerald

http://musicmotivation.com/jeraldsimon
https://facebook.com/jeraldsimon
http://youtube.com/jeraldsimon
http://linkedin.com/in/jeraldsimon
http://pinterest.com/jeraldsimon
https://twitter.com/jeraldsimon
http://cdbaby.com/artist/jeraldsimon
http://instagram.com/jeraldsimon
jeraldsimon@musicmotivation.com

CONTACT Music Motivation®

Music Motivation®
Cool music that excites, entertains, and educates!

Music Motivation®
P.O. Box 1000
Kaysville, UT 84037-1000
http://musicmotivation.com
https://facebook.com/musicmotivation
https://twitter.com/musicmotivation
info@musicmotivation.com

Copyright © 2017 by **Music Motivation**® All Rights Reserved - International Copyright Secured. No part of this book may be copied, reproduced, or duplicated in any form by any mechanical, electronic or other means known or hereafter invented without written permission from the author, Jerald Simon. For more promotional excerpt permission, contact Music Motivation®, **P.O. Box 1000 Kaysville, UT 84037-1000** - jeraldsimon@musicmotivation.com

First Printing 2017 - Printed in the United States of America - 10 9 8 7 6 5 4 3 2 1 - Simon, Jerald - Music Motivation® - Sand Castles - $12.95 US/ $14.95 Canada - Soft cover spiral bound book - ISBN-13: MM00001060

Music Motivation® is a registered ® trademark

Welcome to Sand Castles by JERALD SIMON

All 10 of these cool songs were composed by Jerald Simon as part of his "Cool Songs Individual Piano Student and the Individual and Platinum Piano Teacher packages available on his website (musicmotivation.com)." This is Jerald's description of the Cool Songs he's composed to motivate piano students:

"Jerald Simon composes Cool Songs to teach students the theory of the new piece with fun examples/exercises that demonstrate the practical application of learning music theory, so students can begin making music of their own. Each new Cool Song is emailed to all Music Motivation® mentees according to their preferred subscription."

If you would like to learn more about Jerald's weekly Cool Songs from his annual subscription, you can visit his website at **musicmotivation.com/coolsongs** for more information.

"My purpose and mission in life is to motivate myself and others through my music and writing, to help others find their purpose and mission in life, and to teach values that encourage everyone everywhere to do and be their best." - Jerald Simon

A message from Jerald to piano students and parents:

If you come to piano lessons each week and walk away only having learned about music notation, rhythm, and dots on a page, then I have failed as a Music Mentor. Life lessons are just as important, if not more important than music lessons. I would rather have you learn more about goal setting and achieving, character, dedication, and personal improvement. To have you learn to love music, appreciate it, and play it, is a wonderful byproduct you will have for the rest of your life - a talent that will enrich your life and the lives of others. To become a better musician is wonderful and important, but to become a better person is more important.

As a Music Mentor I want to mentor students to be the very best they can be. If you choose not to practice, you essentially choose not to improve. This is true in any area of life. Everyone has the same amount of time allotted to them. What you choose to do with your time, and where you spend your time, has little to do with the activities being done and more to do with the value attached to each activity.

I believe it's important to be well-rounded and have many diverse interests. I want students to enjoy music, to learn to be creative and understand how to express themselves musically - either by creating music of their own, or interpreting the music of others - by arranging and improvising well known music. In addition, I encourage students to play sports, dance, sing, draw, read, and develop all of their talents. I want them to be more than musicians, I want them to learn to become well-rounded individuals.

Above all, I want everyone to continually improve and do their best. I encourage everyone to set goals, dream big, and be the best they can be in whatever they choose to do. Life is full of wonderful choices. Choose the best out of life and learn as much as you can from everyone everywhere. I prefer being called a Music Mentor because I want to mentor others and help them to live their dreams.

Your life is your musical symphony. Make it a masterpiece!

JERALD SIMON

Copyright © 2017 by Music Motivation® - http://musicmotivation.com

Many piano teachers, piano students, and parents of piano students ask me how or why I began creating the "Cool Songs" from my **"Cool Songs Subscription"** (musicmotivation.com/coolsongs). It began with my "Cool Songs for Cool Kids" Series (Primer Level and Books 1, 2, and 3), and my "Cool Songs that ROCK!" Series (books 1 and 2). To be honest, however, it actually began long before any of those books were created.

I began teaching piano lessons part time in 2003, I was newly married and was selling pianos in a piano store. I didn't start teaching full time as an independent piano teacher until 2006. Between 2003 and 2006 I had a few different sales jobs I did as well, while continuing to do things on the side for my music career. In 2006 I created my music company, **Music Motivation®**, at first for my piano studio and for me as a performing musician. I then felt motivated to come out with two books back to back. The first book I ever created was "An Introduction to Scales and Modes". It is an in-depth tutorial of basic scales and modes in all key signatures. After that I came out with my second book, "Variations on Mary Had a Little Lamb." This book has nine different arrangements I created using the children's song, "Mary Had a Little Lamb." These are some of the arrangements in the book: Mary Took Her Lamb to a Swingin' Jazz Club, Mary's Lamb Had the Blues, Mary Took Her Lamb to a 50s Rock Concert, Mary and Her Lamb Live with Indians, etc., etc., until the last arrangement of: Mary Took Her Lamb to a Funeral.

These books were created to help students learn the theory and the practical application of the music. As a result of these two books, my piano studio more than doubled. At my most busy time in teaching, I had around 88 piano students. The majority were teenage boys (ages 11-19), and most of them wanted to quit piano lessons. Piano teachers and parents of piano students would send me their students who essentially wanted nothing more to do with the instrument. The parents and teachers said they didn't want their students to quit and asked me to try to motivate them to keep playing the piano (I guess that is what I get for naming my company Music Motivation®). The students would not play from any method book past or present and would never suggest music they wanted to play. I needed to figure out how to reach these students and connect with them. I asked each of them what kind of music they enjoyed and asked them to bring it so they could work on it. The majority would not do it. I then asked them to challenge me to create or compose a piano solo for them during their lesson. They all found this very entertaining. I would tell them to choose a style of music, key signature, and the time signature. With some pieces, such as "Game Over" from "Cool Songs for Cool Kids" book 1, they even said I could only use four notes. It was a game for the students and a challenge for me. With each of these students, I composed a piano solo during their lesson time and even notated it in Finale. At the end of their lesson I printed off the music and sent it home with them. I challenged them to learn the piano solo and then let me know what they thought. I told them I would compose a new piece the following week during their next lesson for them.

It worked! The following week, the students returned and I asked them if they had tried to play it. The majority of these students had not only tried to play it, but had perfected the piece and said they were ready to challenge me to compose a new piano solo. I would accept their challenge and tell them they would need to play what I composed. I asked the students what they honestly thought about the music and almost without exception, the students said they thought the music sounded "cool." They told me they would play the piano more if they could have more "cool" sounding music like the piano solo I had composed. I appreciated their positive feedback. I told them I would emphasize the music theory in the "cool song" because they need to know their music theory, but I also told them I wanted them to have fun learning these "cool songs" each week. That is how it all began. All of the "cool songs" I had composed in each lesson were later compiled into "Cool Songs for Cool Kids" books 1, 2, and 3. Because of the great feedback of these books, I then created "Cool Songs that ROCK!" books 1 and 2 for older teenagers that were a little more advanced. I have my students play through all of the "cool songs" I create so I can receive their feedback . They know what they like and what sounds "cool" to them. I listen to and now receive feedback from many piano teachers, piano students, and parents of piano students around the world who tell me what they would like me to compose as well. Have fun with this music!

Copyright © 2017 by Music Motivation® - http://musicmotivation.com

The *Music Motivation* Mentorship Map (for piano students)
by Music Mentor™ Jerald Simon

Music Motivation™
musicmotivation.com

This is only an outline or suggestion - add to it or subtract from it! If you are doing something different all together that works, keep doing it. This is meant to give you ideas and supplement what you're already doing.

	♪ Apprentice ♪ for 1st & 2nd year students	♪ Maestro ♪ for 2nd - 4th year students	♪ Virtuoso ♪ for 3rd year students and above
Repertoire *In addition to the books listed to the right, students can sign up to receive the weekly "Cool Song" and "Cool Exercise" composed by Jerald Simon every week. Visit musicmotivation.com/annualsubscription to learn more and sign up!*	**Music Motivation® Book(s)** What Every Pianist Should Know (Free PDF) Essential Piano Exercises (section 1) The Pentascale Pop Star Cool Songs for Cool Kids (primer level) Cool Songs for Cool Kids (book 1) Songs in Pentascale position: Classical, Jazz, Blues, Popular, Students Choice, Personal Composition (in pentascale position - 5 note piano solo) etc.	**Music Motivation® Book(s)** Essential Piano Exercises (section 2), & New Age An Introduction to Scales and Modes Cool Songs for Cool Kids (book 2) Cool Songs for Cool Kids (book 3) Variations on Mary Had a Little Lamb Twinkle Those Stars, Jazzed about Christmas, Jazzed about 4th of July Baroque, Romantic, Classical, Jazz, Blues, Popular, New Age, Student's Choice, Personal Composition.	**Music Motivation® Book(s)** Essential Piano Exercises (section 3), & Jazz EPE Cool Songs that ROCK! (books 1 & 2) Triumphant, Sea Fever, Sweet Melancholy, The Dawn of a New Age, Sweet Modality, Jazzed about Jazz, Jazzed about Classical Music, Jingle Those Bells, Cinematic Solos, Hymn Arranging Baroque, Romantic, Classical, Jazz, Blues, Popular, New Age, Contemporary, Broadway Show Tunes, Standards, Student's Choice, Personal Composition
Music Terminology	Piano (*p*), Forte (*f*) Mezzo Piano (*mp*) Mezzo Forte (*mf*) Pianissimo (*pp*) Fortissimo (*ff*) *Music Motivation® 1st Year Terminology*	Tempo Markings Dynamic Markings Parts of the Piano Styles and Genres of Music *Music Motivation® 2nd Year Terminology*	Pocket Music Dictionary (2 - 3 years) Harvard Dictionary of Music (4 + years) Parts/History of the Piano Music Composers (Weekly Biographies) *Music Motivation® 3rd Year Terminology*
Key Signatures	C, G, D, A, F, B♭, E♭ & A♭ (Major) A, E, B, F♯, D, G, C & F (Minor) Begin learning all major key signatures	Circle of 5ths/Circle of 4ths All Major and Minor key signatures (Identify each key and name the sharps and flats)	Spiral of Fifths, Chord Progressions within Key Signatures. Modulating from one Key Signature to another.
Music Notation	Names and Positions of notes on the staff (both hands - Treble and Bass Clefs)	Names and Positions of notes above and below the staff (both hands)	History of Music Notation (the development of notation), Monks & Music, Gregorian Chants, Music changes over the years and how music has changed. Learn **Finale** and **Logic Pro** (notate your music)
Rhythms	Whole notes/rests (say it and play it - count out loud) Half notes/rests (say it and play it - count out loud) Quarter notes/rests (say it and play it - count out loud) Eighth notes/rests (say it and play it - count out loud)	Sixteenth notes/rests (say it and play it - count out loud) Thirty-second notes/rests (say it and play it - count out loud) Sixty-fourth notes/rests (say it and play it - count out loud)	One-hundred-twenty-eighth notes/rests For more on rhythm, I recommend: "Rhythmic Training" by Robert Starer and "Logical Approach to Rhythmic Notation" (books 1 & 2) by Phil Perkins
Intervals	1st, 2nd, 3rd, 4th, 5th, 6th, 7th, 8th, and 9th intervals (key of C, G, D, F, B♭, and E♭). Harmonic and Melodic intervals (key of C, G, D, A, E, and B)	All Perfect, Major, Minor, Augmented, and Diminished intervals (in every key). All Harmonic and Melodic intervals. Explain the intervals used to create major, minor, diminished, and augmented chords?	9th, 11th, and 13th intervals. Analyze music (Hymns and Classical) to identify intervals used in each measure. Identify/Name intervals used in chords.
Scales	All Major Pentascales (5 finger scale) All Minor Pentascales (5 finger scale) All Diminished Pentascales (5 finger scale) C Major Scale (1 octave) A min. Scale (1 oct.) (Do, Re, Mi, Fa, Sol, La, Ti, Do) (solfege) All Major and Natural Minor Scales - 1 octave	All Major Scales (Every Key 1 - 2 octaves) All Minor Scales (Every Key 1 - 2 octaves) (natural, harmonic, and melodic minor scales) (Do, Di, Re, Ri, Mi, Fa, Fi, Sol, Si, La, Li, Ti, Do) (solfege - chromatic)	All Major Scales (Every Key 3 - 5 Octaves) All Minor Scales (Every Key 3 - 5 Octaves) All Blues Scales (major and minor) Cultural Scales (25 + scales)
Modes	Ionian/Aeolian (C/A, G/E, D/B, A/F♯)	All Modes (I, D, P, L, M, A, L) All keys	Modulating with the Modes (Dorian to Dorian)
Chords	All Major Chords, All Minor Chords, All Diminished Chords, C Sus 2, C Sus 4, C+ (Aug)., C 6th, C minor 6th, C 7th, C Maj. 7th, C minor Major 7th, A min., A Sus 2, A Sus 4,	All Major, Minor, Diminished, Augmented, Sus 2, Sus 4, Sixth, Minor Sixth, Dominant 7th and Major 7th Chords	Review All Chords from 1st and 2nd year experiences. All 7th, 9th, 11th, and 13th chords inversions and voicings.
Arpeggios	Same chords as above (1 - 2 octaves)	Same chords as above (3 - 4 octaves)	Same chords as above (4 + octaves)
Inversions	Same chords as above (1 - 2 octaves)	Same chords as above (3 - 4 octaves)	Same chords as above (4 + octaves)
Technique (et cetera)	Schmitt Preparatory Exercises, (Hanon)	Wieck, Hanon, Bach (well tempered clavier)	Bertini-Germer, Czerny, I. Philipp
Sight Reading	Key of C Major and G Major	Key of C, G, D, A, E, F, B♭, E♭, A♭, D♭	All Key Signatures, Hymns, Classical
Ear Training	Major versus Minor sounds (chords/intervals)	C, D, E, F, G, A, B, and intervals	Key Signatures and Chords, Play w/ IPod
Music History	The origins of the Piano Forte	Baroque, Classical, Jazz, Blues	Students choice - All genres, Composers
Improvisation	Mary Had a Little Lamb, Twinkle, Twinkle...	Blues Pentascale, Barrelhouse Blues	Classical, New Age, Jazz, Blues, etc. Play w/ IPod
Composition	5 note melody (both hands - key of C and G)	One - Two Page Song (include key change)	Lyrical, Classical, New Age, Jazz, etc.

The books from the Music Motivation® Series by Jerald Simon are not method books, and are not intentionally created to be used as such (although some piano teachers use them as such). Jerald simply creates fun, cool piano music to motivate piano students to play the piano and teach them music theory - the FUN way!

Copyright © 2004 - 2015 by Music Motivation® All Rights Reserved

A few theory FUNdamentals to work on! (practice these)

First, I'd like to have you try to play all perfect fifth intervals moving up in half steps as shown in the example below:

These are all perfect 5th intervals moving up in half steps chromatically (in half steps) through every key signature:

same fingering on every perfect 5th interval

same fingering on every perfect 5th interval

Now, try playing all octave intervals moving up in half steps as shown in this example:

These are all 8th or octave intervals moving up in half steps chromatically (in half steps) through every key signature:

same fingering on every 8th (or octave) interval

same fingering on every 8th (or octave) interval

The example below shows measures 1-4 from the piano piece "Sand Castles" on page 10. It is in a 4/4 time signature in the key of C Major. This left hand pattern is a 1 - 5 - 8 - 9 - 10 - 9 left hand pattern. Try playing this left hand pattern starting on every key on the piano so you can play this in all key signatures.

Delicately (M.M. ♩ = c. 70)

Ped. ad lib

Copyright © 2017 by Music Motivation® - http://musicmotivation.com

MM00001060

A few theory FUNdamentals to work on! (practice these)

The example below shows measures 1-4 from the piano piece "Forsaken" on page 23. It is in a 4/4 time signature. This piece is in the key of F minor (relative minor to A flat Major). Play the example below.

Now play all of the triads created from the C Major scale (all in root position) moving up the scale. You have C Major, D minor, E minor, F Major, G Major, A minor, B diminished, and C Major. The left hand is playing the accompanying perfect 5th interval that relates to the triad played with the right hand.

Pretty easy, huh? Now that you can play that, try to *play the exact same six measures from above in all key signatures.* You can follow the **Circle of 5ths, the circle/cycle of 4ths,** or simply move up chromatically in half steps. Since we are using the triads created from the major scale, let's start off by following the **Circle of 5ths.** This then becomes your order for the key signatures you will play (these are not chords, but are the corresponding key signatures and order in which to use them):

C Major - G Major - D Major - A Major - E Major - B Major - F sharp Major - C sharp Major

Going backwards you can follow the **Circle/Cycle of 4ths** as follows:

C Major - F Major - B flat Major - E flat Major - A flat Major - D flat Major - G flat Major - C flat Major

The whole point of this exercise is to have you try to transpose a few measures and play the same thing in all key signatures without looking at the music. You can do this. If you take the exercise above and play it in the key of G Major, as an example, the order of your triads played with the right hand would be:

G Major, A minor, B minor, C Major, D Major, E minor, F sharp diminished, G Major

Try to play this in all keys. Have fun with this!

Copyright © 2017 by Music Motivation® - http://musicmotivation.com

ARISE

Skill - We are in the key of C Major. The right hand primarily plays a perfect fifth and perfect fourth interval - alternating between the two intervals. Starting in measure 15 the left hand moves in fifth intervals.

JERALD SIMON

Sweetly and Tenderly ♩ = 75

Copyright © 2017 by Music Motivation® - http://musicmotivation.com
All Rights Controlled and Administered by ASCAP
International Copyright Secured
All rights reserved including the right of public performance for profit

MM00001060

To learn more about Jerald's cool songs and cool exercises, please visit musicmotivation.com/coolsongs

Copyright © 2017 by Music Motivation® - http://musicmotivation.com

Sand Castles

Skill - Left hand pattern: 1 - 5 - 8 - 9 - 10 - 9 (try this starting on every key on the piano)

JERALD SIMON

Delicately (M.M. ♩ = c. 70)

Copyright © 2017 by Music Motivation® - http://musicmotivation.com
All Rights Controlled and Administered by ASCAP
International Copyright Secured
All rights reserved including the right of public performance for profit

MM00001060

Copyright © 2017 by Music Motivation® - http://musicmotivation.com

Summer Nights

Skill - Students learn the sharps in the F# major key signature, the F# major scale, and also learn how to compose a "Cool Song" of their own using the F# tetra-chord (F#, G#, A#, and B). To learn more, watch the video of Summer Nights on youtube.com/jeraldsimon

Like you're playing night games! (M.M. ♩ = c. 120)

JERALD SIMON

Copyright © 2017 by Music Motivation® - http://musicmotivation.com
All Rights Controlled and Administered by ASCAP
International Copyright Secured
All rights reserved including the right of public performance for profit

MM00001060

Summer Nights

Copyright © 2017 by Music Motivation® - http://musicmotivation.com

ETHEREAL

Skill - Students learn the harmonic intervals from the key of D major (created from the D major scale)
To learn more, watch the video of Ethereal on youtube.com/jeraldsimon

JERALD SIMON

Powerful, yet subdued (M.M. ♩ = c. 120)

Copyright © 2017 by Music Motivation® - http://musicmotivation.com
All Rights Controlled and Administered by ASCAP
International Copyright Secured
All rights reserved including the right of public performance for profit

MM00001060

ETHEREAL

MM00001060   Copyright © 2017 by Music Motivation® - http://musicmotivation.com

SUMMER SUNRISE

Skill - Students learn the 1-5-8 (see measure 1) and 1-5-8-9-10 (see measures 6-9) new age left hand patterns with this piece. This coolsong is in the key of A flat major and the students see the A flat major scale incorporated into the music (see measure 4). To learn more, watch the video of Summer Sunrise on youtube.com/jeraldsimon

JERALD SIMON

Meaningfully (M.M. ♩ = c. 75)

Copyright © 2017 by Music Motivation® - http://musicmotivation.com
All Rights Controlled and Administered by ASCAP
International Copyright Secured
All rights reserved including the right of public performance for profit

MM00001060

To learn more about Jerald's cool songs and cool exercises, please
visit musicmotivation.com/coolsongs

MM00001060

Copyright © 2017 by Music Motivation® - http://musicmotivation.com

Flip-side

Skill - We are in the key of D minor which is the relative minor to F Major. The purpose of this "Cool Song" is to help students learn the primary minor cadence of the i-iv-V chord progression in the key of D minor. Students also learn about sixth intervals starting in measure 7 and are shown a simple ostinato left hand pattern beginning in measure 13. Have FUN playing this "Cool Song"!

JERALD SIMON

Artistically - with a classical flair ♩ = 100

This is the fingering I use, but please use what is best for your hand size.

Copyright © 2017 by Music Motivation® - http://musicmotivation.com
All Rights Controlled and Administered by ASCAP
International Copyright Secured
All rights reserved including the right of public performance for profit

MM00001060

Flip-side

MM00001060

Copyright © 2017 by Music Motivation® - http://musicmotivation.com

Daylight

Skill - We are in the key of F Major. This piece has quite a bit of movement up and down the piano. Keep a very gentle and tender feeling about the piece as you play it. It should feel like light entering a room. Try to compose a "Cool Song" of your own like this. Have FUN playing this "Cool Song"!

rubato - play freely throughout the piece
(don't worry about staying with a tempo - play with feeling)

JERALD SIMON

Tenderly and Thoughtfully (M.M. ♩ = c. 85)

Copyright © 2017 by Music Motivation® - http://musicmotivation.com
All Rights Controlled and Administered by ASCAP
International Copyright Secured
All rights reserved including the right of public performance for profit

MM00001060

Daylight

MM00001060   Copyright © 2017 by Music Motivation® - http://musicmotivation.com   **21**

Daylight

Copyright © 2017 by Music Motivation® - http://musicmotivation.com

MM00001060

Forsaken

Skill - We are in the key of F minor which is the relative minor to A flat Major. This piece is also using the 4/4 time signature. Watch what the right hand does throughout the piece. I played this at 106 when I filmed it/recorded it, but you can play anywhere between 90 and 112. Have FUN playing this "Cool Song"!

Tenderly and Thoughtfully (M.M. ♩ = c. 90-112)

JERALD SIMON

Copyright © 2017 by Music Motivation® - http://musicmotivation.com
All Rights Controlled and Administered by ASCAP
International Copyright Secured
All rights reserved including the right of public performance for profit

MM00001060

Forsaken

Copyright © 2017 by Music Motivation® - http://musicmotivation.com

MM00001060

Forsaken

Copyright © 2017 by Music Motivation® - http://musicmotivation.com

Twirling

Skill - We are in the key of C Major. The most challenging aspect about this "Cool Song" is the time signature. Keep a constant 5/4 feel. It makes you feel as if you are twirling while you play it. Have FUN playing this "Cool Song"!

JERALD SIMON

With a gentle lilt (M.M. ♩ = c. 85)

Copyright © 2017 by Music Motivation® - http://musicmotivation.com
All Rights Controlled and Administered by ASCAP
International Copyright Secured
All rights reserved including the right of public performance for profit

MM00001060

Easy Does It!

Skill - We are in the key of D Major. This is a fun, easy going piece. The left hand primarily plays perfect fifth and major sixth intervals. Can you identify all of them? Students can write in their own dynamic markings with this piece! Have FUN playing this "Cool Song"!

Pop Ballad Feel (M.M. ♩ = c. 110)

JERALD SIMON

Ped. ad lib
Students can write in their own dynamic markings with this piece!

Copyright © 2017 by Music Motivation® - http://musicmotivation.com
All Rights Controlled and Administered by ASCAP
International Copyright Secured
All rights reserved including the right of public performance for profit

MM00001060

Easy Does It!

To learn more about Jerald's cool songs and cool exercises, please
visit musicmotivation.com/coolsongs

Copyright © 2017 by Music Motivation® - http://musicmotivation.com

Testimonials about Jerald
here are a few testimonials from musicians and piano teachers

"Jerald's hymn arrangements are as beautiful as they are musically interesting. I'm sure people are going to love hearing them in church meetings or wherever they are played."

- Jon Schmidt - Piano Guys

"Jerald is a wonderful human being who has inspired not only me to be a better pianist, but hundreds of other people. Keep up all the great work Jerald."

- Paul Cardall - Music Producer, Film Composer, Recording Artist

"What I love about arrangements of well-sung songs done by various artists is that one can hear the pianist's personality come through in a very real and intimate way. Jerald's passion for life and his beliefs comes through in his unique and distinctive arrangements of these well-known religious hymns."

- Kurt Bestor (Owner, Kurt Bestor Music)

"Jerald Simon's arrangement of A Poor Wayfaring Man of Grief is peaceful and soothing. It is not rushed, allowing lines to breathe and resolve. He continues to produce music that will bring spiritual comfort to those who are listening."

- Josh Wright (concert pianist and online piano teacher)

"Jerald Simon is a brilliant musician, teacher, and performer, with a fascinating story to tell. If you're interested in learning how to improvise or compose music, be sure to check out his books."

- Brandon Pearce - Owner, Music Teacher's Helper, LLC

"Jerald's motivational poetry, writing and music education books are a true expression of Jerald's winning personality and innovation. He is a Utah treasure."

- David Burger, Music critic, arts reporter, Salt Lake Tribune

"Not only do you get a song per week to learn, but all of the "fixings" (supplements) to go with it! Backing tracks, PDFs and also a step by step video going though each song. Wow! It's a great value for the price. I think students would enjoy playing these (cool) songs. Teachers and students shouldn't think twice about learning about (Jerald's) compositions and letting themselves be inspired by his musical style. Don't delay - jump in today!"

- Jeff Willie - Piano Teacher

"My favorite thing about the "Cool Songs" is the music theory that is introduced in the YouTube videos. So many times, students don't understand the why behind theory until they have been taking lessons for several years. The videos introduce theory concepts in a way that compliments the song, and then gives students a reason to actually use it!" Thanks again!

-Amanda W Smith (Piano Teacher - Founder of modernmusicteaching.com

 Copyright © 2017 by Music Motivation® - http://musicmotivation.com

Jerald's Albums & Singles
are available from all online music stores

Jerald continually produces and releases new "Cool Songs" available for all piano students and piano teachers on his website (*musicmotivation.com*). Each new "*Cool Song*" is emailed to Music Motivation® mentees (piano teachers and piano students) according to their preferred subscription. See which subscription is the best fit for you and for your piano students (if you are a piano teacher) by visiting:

http://musicmotivation.com/coolsongs

At Music Motivation®, I strive to produce the best quality products I can to help musicians of all ages better understand music theory (Theory Therapy), improvisation (Innovative Improvisation), and composition (Creative Composition). I try to tailor my products around the needs of piano teachers and piano students of all ages - from beginning through advanced and would love to receive your feedback about what I can do to better help you teach and learn. Let me know if there is a type of piano music, music book, fun audio or video tutorial, or any other educational product you would like to see in the field of music (principally the piano), but have not yet found, that would help you teach and learn the piano better. Please contact me. I look forward to your comments and suggestions. Thank you.

Check out these best sellers by Jerald Simon

Jerald is continually coming out with new books and has multiple books planned to be released each year. Check musicmotivation.com for new books, CD, singles, and more.

visit *musicmotivation.com* to purchase, or visit your local music store - Chesbro music is the national distributor for all Music Motivation® books. Contact Chesbro Music Co. if you are a store (1.800.243.7276)

Learn more about
JERALD SIMON

Visit **http://musicmotivation.com/jeraldsimon**

"My purpose and mission in life is to motivate myself and others through my music and writing, to help others find their purpose and mission in life, and to teach values and encourage everyone everywhere to do and be their best." - Jerald Simon

First and foremost, Jerald is a husband to his beautiful wife, Zanny, and a father to his wonderful children. Jerald Simon is the founder and president of Music Motivation® (**musicmotivation.com**). He is a composer, author, poet, and Music Mentor/piano teacher (primarily focusing his piano teaching on music theory, and encouraging students with improvisation, composition, and arranging). Jerald loves music, teaching, speaking, performing, playing sports, exercising, gardening (he's a wannabe gardener) reading, writing poetry and self help books, and spending time with his wife, Zanny, and their children.

Jerald created **musicmotivation.com** as a resource for piano teachers, piano students, and parents of piano students. He is the author/poet of "The As If Principle" (222 motivational poems), and "Perceptions, Parables, and Pointers." He is also the author of 20 music books from the Music Motivation® Series (over 200 plus original piano solos between the books) including the popular series: Cool Songs for Cool Kids (pre-primer, primer level, and volumes 1, 2, and 3) and Cool Songs that Rock (books 1 and 2) which all feature original piano music Jerald has composed primarily with teenage boys in mind. He has also recorded and produced several albums and singles of original music as well as hymn arrangements. In 2014, Jerald started a "Cool Songs" annual subscription on his website where he produces and releases one new "Cool Song" for the piano every week with minus tracks (accompaniment parts), the PDF download, MP3 downloads, and a YouTube video tutorial where he teaches the "Cool Song" and music theory the fun way. Watch his videos on his website at http://musicmotivation.com/coolsongs, and check out his videos at http://youtube.com/jeraldsimon

Jerald also presents to various music schools, groups, and associations throughout the country doing various workshops, music camps, master classes, concerts and firesides to inspire and motivate teens, adults, music students and teachers. He enjoys teaching piano students about music theory, improvisation, and composition. He refers to himself as a Music Mentor and encourages music students to get motivated by music and to motivate others through music of their own.

SPECIALTIES:

Composer, Author, Poet, Music Mentor, Piano Teacher (jazz, music theory, improvisation, composition, arranging, etc.), Motivational Speaker, and life coach. Visit **http://musicmotivation.com**, to book Jerald as a speaker/performer. Visit **http://musicmotivation.com** to print off FREE piano resources for piano teachers and piano students.

www.ingramcontent.com/pod-product-compliance
Lightning Source LLC
LaVergne TN
LVHW061342060426
835511LV00014B/2065

9 781948 274005